Sell More Easily:
Tales From The Trenches Guaranteed to Make You More Money

By Howard Maslich, MA

I want to thank my daughter Meredith without whom this book would never have come to fruition. It is Meredith's creative drive, editing skills and unyielding confidence that has made this book possible.

Contents

INTRODUCTION

My Story

It was 1971, and I was 22 years old with long hair, wide chops and a full beard. I was an assistant professor of psychology at a junior college, and I was in the midst of the youthful counter culture milieu, sitting at a registration table in the gymnasium during course registration. The line of students for psychology and humanities courses was so long it wound outside the gym and onto the street. The lines for the business and engineering courses were much shorter. I and the other humanities professors almost felt bad for those poor teachers, struggling to get enough students to fill their classes. But, not that bad; after all it *was* the early 70's, and humanism seemed a most healthy rebellion against the military industrial complex that got us into Vietnam and generally created the soulless, existential vacuum, of the corporate man.

I continued to ride high on this wave of liberal intellectualism until the fall registration of 1975 when the inevitable pendulum of life began to swing in the other direction. The lines in the gym at that semester's sign up reversed and we humanities dudes found ourselves begging for students, while the business and engineering departments had lines out to the street. It seemed that the counter culture rebellion had fizzled out and now, young people wanted jobs that paid. The American dream was alive and well again. For me, that meant something called "retrenchment" a word I quickly learned meant that, since there weren't enough students for me to teach, I was fired.

The golden years of classes, filled with starry eyed coeds hanging on my every word of enlightened wisdom had come to a screeching halt. Now I was looking at the fish eye of the unemployment lady once a week as she said "Have you looked for work this week?" and I would reply "Of course." It wasn't a total lie because I had collected a library of 24 books representing information on available vocations, from bank president to pharmacist. The time began to run out for collecting my unemployment checks and every profession I studied seemed to lack something. Then my beautiful wife presented me with the birth of my gorgeous daughter. Responsibility was beginning to press upon me and I began to feel the approach of a large wheel, rolling toward me. I didn't want to get crushed beneath it. As fate would have it, an old teaching colleague of mine recommended that I visit with one of my former continuing education students, Ed, who was now in some kind of consulting business because maybe he could help me find some work. Ed's office was in his home. He greeted me at the door and proceeded to lead me through a nicely appointed hallway toward his home office, which seemed to have once been a den. Once inside the office Ed slid himself comfortably behind a large executive style oak desk and gestured for me to take the seat as he proceeded to say, "Howard, you are a very good teacher. I enjoyed your class very much, but you can make a whole lot more money in the training business, teaching people how to sell."

He then laid out fifty checks made out to him from different companies he had sold sales training to. The total of these checks was something in the neighborhood of $95,000. Remember, this was in 1976. His next question took me about 4 seconds to answer "Howard, would you like to learn how I do this and join me?"

Well, the rest- as they say- is history, and for the last forty years I have been enjoying a very comfortable living as a result of that meeting. When you learn and practice the principles, tactics and strategies I will teach you in this book, you will be capable of getting anything you want, from anybody.

Who Should Read This Book

If you are a new or struggling salesperson, this book will introduce you to a whole new approach to selling and help you overcome any self-limiting fears or beliefs that are holding you back.

If you are an experienced salesperson, this book will help you to refresh your perspective, give you some new ideas, and help you advance in the art of sales.

After you have read this book you will be able to: use basic concepts of human psychology to understand how to build relationships, how to get to the real motivation for a prospect's interest in buying (or for not buying!), how to break through common stalls and objections, how to get the best possible price for your product or service and. You will learn to love the game of selling!

Even if you aren't a salesperson at all, this book will help you to negotiate your next raise and to win arguments with your spouse or your children.

FOUNDATIONS OF THE SELL MORE EASILY SYSTEM

Assumptions

Before we get started, I want to share some assumptions I am making about you. I'm assuming that you sell something for a living, that you want to start selling for a living, or that you have a desire to be more persuasive in some other human endeavor. Secondly, I'm assuming that what you sell, or that the reason you want to persuade someone, is ultimately for a good purpose.

Either way, the process begins by learning a systematic selling process. The selling system you will learn here has five steps: Rapport – Pain – Money – Commitment – Close.

Overview of Selling System

Before you start to learn the steps, you have to learn how to qualify a prospect. A qualified prospect is someone who has need (Pain), resources (Money), ability and willingness to spend those resources (Commitment).

But before you can qualify your prospects, you have to get in front of prospective prospects. And for most sales people, myself included, that means cold calling.

When I started out I was selling sales training door to door. Our target market was local small businesses and since there were lots of them there was no shortage of places to call upon. Making thousands of cold calls to get started would have been a very daunting task if it wasn't for the system I learned.

I learned that cold calls are divided into two categories: Boss Talks and Chalk Talks. The Boss Talks are aimed at finding the decision maker and qualifying him or her through three core steps of the process: Pain, Money and Commitment.

The Chalk Talks are the "Solution Presentation" and result in the decision which either closed the sale or closed the file on that prospect. The solution presentation occurs when the prospect has been shown how they'd be helped. In principle, you need to help them believe that you have the fix for their pain within their budget. In terms of method the salesperson does whatever it takes to bring that prospect to conviction. It might be a power point, a written proposal or a verbal conversation. The method is not important, only that the prospect perceives that you can take his pain away with your product.

Dividing the calls into two steps helped me tremendously. Back in those days there were no white boards in conference rooms, or laptops and portable projectors for power point presentations. I used to schlep around a news print easel with telescoping legs as my presentation tool, complete with a set of fat, smelly, markers. The only problem was, I was making all these calls in office buildings, coming in with a 36" X 24" easel and asking the receptionist if Mike Smith the President was in. It was a little over the top!

This is where the two categories of calls comes in. The first call was the Boss Talk and it was made with nothing; I call it the naked cold call because I didn't bring the easel, or brochures, or a briefcase or even a business card. It sounds crazy, I know. Everyone thinks they'll look unprofessional, or unprepared or just plain stupid if they go in "naked" but, this is an important part of the strategy because on the Boss Talk, I wanted the Boss to do all the talking. I wanted to just listen and be able to start qualifying her through the three steps.

First, does she have Pain? Does she have a problem that is disturbing her to the point that she is feeling psychological pain? Second, does she have Money? Is she willing and able to spend money to fix this problem? And third, Commitment. Is she willing and able to make the decision to spend the money, to fix the problem to end the pain?

That was it for the first meeting. If I got through these three steps, I earned the right to a second meeting. That was when I appeared, easel in hand, to set up in front of the Boss's face and begin my wiz bang presentation with my multi colored markers. (Although, in reality, I mostly used black because I became paralyzed trying to decide which color marker I should use to emphasize what point.) At the end of my solution presentation, which was designed to show the boss how I was going to train his salespeople to fix all the problems (solve all his pain) that he'd identified during our initial Boss Talk. At the end of the presentation the boss would give me his yes or no.

So, to summarize: the first call was naked, and only those that qualified got a second call with presentation and either we did business or it was over. Like any good, slightly obsessive sales person, I kept meticulous numbers (with the help of my wife, Carole) and the results were very interesting. After the first 2000 calls (no, that's not a misprint, there isn't an extra zero, I made 2000 cold calls in those first four months. The ratios kept coming up 10 – 3 -1 meaning every 10 first calls produced 3 qualified second solution calls and every three solution calls closed 1 sale. So after 2000 cold calls I made 200 sales and was on my way to building a business.

That close ratio was the result of carefully working the five steps of the Sell More Easily System – Pain, Money, Commitment, Close, on carefully qualified prospects. If I'd worked the system on unqualified prospects, I would probably still have made a few lucky closes. Conversely, if I qualified the prospects, but then didn't stick to the steps of the system carefully, I probably would have also closed a few sales. But my close ratio, a close rate that let me rapidly build a strong business that allowed me to provide a nice home, cars, and vacations for my family, and still put two children through college (one to a very pricey private school), was the direct result of carefully following every step of the system, as well as fully understanding the psychology and philosophy behind the steps, which we'll talk about in the second half of this book. But first, we start by learning the steps.

LEARNING THE STEPS

Rapport

Selling is - at the most basic level - simply a conversation between two people. I have found that generally, what is typically called a conversation is really just an exchange of monologues. A sales conversation needs to be based on a connection and an interconnection between the people involved.

St. Augustine once said that one should seek to understand before one seeks to be understood. I believe this statement is the underlying principle of good communication and specifically, of excellent selling. Perhaps you have had the experience of relating to someone an emotional experience that had an impact on you, and what you heard back was something inadequate like "oh wow" and then the person proceeds to tell you a long story about something that happened to them. Now maybe in the loosest of definitions this passes for empathy but in my opinion it certainly doesn't come up to the standard of St. Augustine's definition of seek to understand before you seek to be understood.

The sales process begins with establishing "rapport": a relationship of mutual trust or affinity, building a connection between you and the person you want to sell to. Are you familiar with the Greek Myth of Narcissus? Basically this dude, Narcissus, looks into a pond, sees his reflection and falls in love with himself. You and I do that every morning when we look in the bathroom mirror right? Okay, maybe love is a bit strong and the entire field of psychiatry would disappear if we all *really* loved ourselves. So I'll bring it down to the level of "comfortable with oneself". I am sure you will agree that you are more comfortable with yourself than you are with anyone else. So the myth of Narcissus tells us that if you are communicating with a stranger it works best if you help them to feel like you are just like them. One way to accomplish this is to employ a strategy perfected by Richard Bandler, the creator of the school of psychology known as Neuro-Linguistic Programming, or NLP. The strategy is called *mirror, match, pace and then lead*.

Mirroring and matching the prospect means, copying their observable behavior like body language, including facial expressions, movement of hands, arms, head tilt etc. **Pacing** is when you match their speed of talking, their tonality and their mood. So if they are speaking fast and excitedly, you would increase the pace of your speech and increase your energy level. After you Mirror, match and pace the other person for a while you can begin to *lead* them where you want them to go. If you start to slow your pace, they will unconsciously start to slow theirs too. If they have been leaning toward you during the conversation, and you lean back they will most likely follow, and relax back into a slower and more focused conversation.

We are talking about the most powerful and quickest way to develop rapport with anyone, anytime, anywhere and it's the deepest level of bonding because it is unconscious. There are other ways of building a connection between you and the person you want to sell or persuade, but this one is simple and elegant. Practice by observing the behavior of people around you. See what they do with their bodies and what words they use when talking. For example a prospect may say "I can't really *see* how this product will help me" and the salesperson's matching reply might be "You can't *see* how this product will help you? Ok, what do you *see*?" People take in information through eyes, ears and touch, each sense has a certain language that goes with it. The eyes see, the ears hear and the fingers touch and feel. Listen for these words because that tells you how your prospect likes to take in information and matching those words will create rapport even faster. After observing for a while, try to pace and mirror and finally lead by changing your body language and notice if the person follows you. Once a warm connection is made you are ready for the next important step in the selling process.

Pain

Selling, like a true conversation, is about hearing, listening and really trying hard to understand what the person is telling you about their world. The trained salesperson is listening with a professionally trained ear. In my world that means listening for the pain and the reasons for the pain and how the pain is impacting the person and the person's business. The underlying principle is that people buy to avoid or eliminate pain.

If we look at the selling process from a psychological point of view we can borrow the Freudian model for a moment. According to Freud, human behavior is based on a tension reduction model, which means, biological or psychological drives create tension within a person and the tension will continue to build until the drive is satisfied. Once the drive is satisfied, homeostasis, or a steady balanced state, is once again achieved. The tension-reduction process is easily illustrated with an example of the hunger drive. When you first become hungry the *Id*, or pleasure center of the brain, creates mental images of food. You may start thinking about where you want to have lunch or what you will make for yourself when you get home. As the hunger tension builds your thinking focuses more and more on the food until that's all you can think about. When finally you eat something the tension is reduced and homeostatic balance is once more temporarily achieved, and you are able to think about something other than eating.

The process is similar with all types of tangible and intangible purchases that people make. If I am hot in my home on a summer day I will stand it for a certain amount of time until I must go out and purchase an air-conditioner to achieve the balance of comfort I seek. So, whatever it is you are selling, first determine what the pain of not having it looks like to the person and gauge how much tension they are feeling and know that the more pain they have, the more tension they have, the more likely this person is to take some sort of action to reduce the tension and get back to a steady state. Hence the principle, people buy ways to eliminate or avoid pain. Incidentally tension reduction is about as close to happiness as one gets, according to Freud.

Your job is to learn exactly what problems your product or service can remove for your prospects. Once you identify the full range of problems that you can solve with your product lines or different services, the next task is to determine how disturbed they are by the problems. This step of the system is called **Pain.** People buy for one of 2 reasons:

1. They want to eliminate pain they have now or,

2. They want to avoid some future pain that they can see.

In this step you are asking questions and learning whether the prospect has a problem you can fix and just how disturbed by the problem they are. Without Pain you are going nowhere.

Another way to phrase this is in the negative "people don't buy either because they don't have a problem or they have a problem but they just aren't disturbed enough to do anything about it at the present time."

The system you are learning in this book is based on a "solution selling" model. There are big margins in providing solutions rather than selling commodities. If you begin to see yourself as a problem solver, rather than a salesperson, your success, and thus, income will immediately improve.

Working the Pain

When you are looking for pain during your prospecting interview you will want to keep a few principles in mind. First, finding pain is always a process of "drilling down" – or getting below the surface, and then below that level until you hit the bottom – which is the full and truest level of the problem or pain.

Start with uncovering the problem, which we will call the WHAT. The next level down is the *reasons* for the problem that the prospect is aware of. This level is called the WHY, and for our purposes the WHY is more important than the WHAT because when a prospect begins to tell you the details of his problem and his perception of why he is experiencing the problem, this tells you that the problem may be real. The third level down, in the pursuit of real pain is the *impact* of the problem on the person and the business. This the HOW, as in, "How does this problem impact your business?" At the third impact level you must help the prospect to quantify his problem. You will find that most business problems have a cost to them. I sometimes call this "pain by the numbers". This step is very important because it goes a long way to creating concrete monetary value of return on investment. Most problems in business can be fixed for 10% of the cost of the problem. So if xyz corporation has a 1M problem that your product or service can solve, on average it will cost 100K to fix it.

Practice finding pain by setting up a chart. In the left hand margin write "product or service". The next column should be labeled "Feature", the next "Benefit" the next "Pain". In the first column write down the names of all the product lines that you sell, then list the prominent features of each product then the benefit to the customer and finally the problem (pain) that the product benefit is designed to eliminate.

Once you have completed this chart you can begin to formulate your pain interview questions. So for example, if you sell e-commerce consulting services, one feature might be knowledge about computers, internet and social media. The benefit would be "we can help you enter the ecommerce business environment." Pain might be I get no business from the internet and have fear of it. So one pain question could be "How much business are your competitors who are using the internet getting, that you are missing?"

Practice interviewing for pain and then match your best product/service solution. Utilizing this approach will also differentiate you from the competition since they will all be pitching features and benefits and sounding the same. For example, in my town as probably in yours, there are five number one radio stations.

That is what the small business person trying to buy radio advertising thinks after hearing the five pitches that all sound the same and present evidence as to why they are number one. In today's economy there are too many sellers selling the same thing the same way. Differentiate yourself by using the solution selling model and interviewing the prospect for pain. **If your competition is doing it you must stop doing it and do it a different way to increase market share.**

Money

Once you have moved through all of the levels of pain and developed at least one that goes all the way down to the bottom, you are ready for the next step of the system - the MONEY Step.

The primary objective when qualifying the prospect in the money step is the determination of the *Willingness* and *Ability* of the prospect to pay the amount of money required to solve their problem. Our friends Will and Able must travel together because Will to pay without ability is a non-starter and Able to pay but not willing to give it to you is also no good. So, we qualify the prospect's willingness to pay and make sure they also have the ability. I sometimes call this step the "Show Me the Money" step. Reference here to Cuba Gooding Jr. screaming at his agent Jerry Mcquire!! A very important concept in the money step is what I call the HPP: the Highest Plausible Price.

Every sales transaction has an HPP. The research shows that what the salesperson thinks is the HPP number is usually lower than what the HPP actually is. In other words most salespeople err by leaving money on the table. Money is an interesting issue and is laden with emotionally conditioned attitudes that can limit a salesperson's ability to ask for lots of money. The rule is: *The salesperson will get as much money as they are strong enough to ask for.* Many salespeople are trapped in money comfort zones that limit their ability to actualize the HPP of a sales transaction. It is essential to buy into the problem – pain – solution model in order to believe how much you are helping the prospect eliminate his problems and what that is worth monetarily to him. Once you begin thinking this way you will start to increase your confidence to ask for larger orders at higher prices.

Money is an emotion laden concept with self-limiting beliefs that manifest as mental traps. For example, answer this question; How much money is a lot of money to you? If your answer is in the millions you have a high money concept. If you answered in the hundreds you have a low money concept. In the old days the sales trainers used to call it "selling out of your pocket." When the salesperson judges whether a prospect can afford to pay for the product or service he is selling based on whether he can afford it himself. The salesperson projects her money concept into the wallet of the potential customer. Hence, the rule "In sales you will get as much money as you are strong enough to ask for."

Many of my clients, these days, are very concerned about margins. What I find when auditing a sales force is that margins are all over the place based on the internal self-limiting beliefs that the salesperson harbors. Since these beliefs are often unconscious, the person will not be aware of them and will blame the low margins on externals such as, the product, the market, the management, etc. My research and experience tells me that the low margin problem is a state of mind. Once liberated from these toxic money attitudes I have seen salespeople increase their margins dramatically and never go back.

Commitment

The Commitment step is the place where the salesperson learns who the decision makers are, when they will make the decision, and what process they will use to make it. The key in this step, as in all the others, is to qualify hard so you get the truth. The goal is to make sure, when it comes time for closing, that all the relevant decision makers are present. As with the other qualifying steps in the system, when a sale does not close it is because one of the steps was not worked hard or well enough, and this step is no exception.

The unique feature of the Commitment step is the "deal before the deal," as one of my clients put it. This means that the prospect must make a commitment to you *now* that he will in fact make a yes or no decision *later,* after he experiences your solution presentation.

Now occasionally the prospect would forget that they had made a commitment to say "YES" or "NO". After all, the agreement was made with a salesman and, even St Peter will open the pearly gates if you only lie to a salesman. When the prospect reverts and says "MAYBE" we've come to a fork in the road! This is where the courage of conviction is tested. There is only one correct response and that is to remind the prospect of the agreement to say "YES" or "NO" and to help them to say "NO"!

It sounds like this: "Mr. Prospect, you and I agreed that you would either accept or reject my proposal and that is our first important commitment to each other. If we break the first one how can we have faith in all the commitments we will be making together in the future? If you're saying 'Maybe' that means, to me, that you don't want to say Yes so why don't you say No and we can end it here?"

In one case where this happened, the prospect said "But I don't want to say NO" and I said "Well then, what is stopping you from saying Yes" and the prospect mentioned two small objections, that I handled, easily and the sale was closed." Of course you know what the Wimp move sounds like - "Okay, I will call you next week." The Wimp salesperson goes into endless follow up that wastes time and leads nowhere near the bank.

When the commitment step is weak, instead of hearing YES or NO at the end of your solution presentation you will hear things like: "This is great, I love it but it's not my decision", or "Wow, wait until I tell my boss about this. I will get back to you soon", or "I don't think my boss would go for this", or "Let me check this out with our committee." These are statements you don't want to hear, because no matter how wonderful your closing presentation is or how great your product or service, the people in the room cannot make the commitment to buy.

I remember when I called on Rothsfeld Jewelers and I was talking with John Rothsfeld. We worked through the first three steps of the system, **Rapport, Pain and Money**. When we got to **Commitment,** I assumed it was an automatic, because I was talking with John Rothsfeld - the name on the sign in front of the store. At the end of the presentation I asked for the Yes or No decision and this is what I heard: "Howard I would love to do it but I have to check with my father Ted Engleberg who is the owner and the boss, I will get back to you and thanks so much for your time." I didn't get a decision, but I did get two very important lessons: Never assume ANYTHING, and the sale is NEVER closed, until it's closed. Never skip or short change a step in the process,

Those fork in the road moments come up at this step as well and I remember another incident when the Boss and Sales Manager were qualified in the first meeting. When I showed up with my trusty easel after driving seventy miles I looked at the sales manager and said "Hi Bob where is Charles"? And Bob said "Oh he couldn't make it but he wants us to go ahead with the presentation and I can fill him in later." Well, I was immediately deflated. I had driven seventy miles and was all hyped up with excited expectations about closing a sale. The wrong thing to do in this situation, which is what I have done many times, is to present anyway. Most of the time, you end up in "follow up forever land" with no sale. Since I had finally internalized that lesson at this point in my career, I looked thoughtfully at the sales manager, easel under my arm, and said "You know Bob, we had an agreement that I would be presenting to you and your boss and I would prefer to stick to the agreement and reschedule for when he can make it." He agreed to reschedule, and at the end of that meeting, the sale was closed.

You know when you hear about the tragic event of a plane crashing and after the investigation it's learned that the reason was pilot error? That's generally the reason sales crash: salesperson error. The important thing is to take full responsibility for the reason your sale doesn't close. Almost every time it's going to be because you decided you could go against the system, or short cut the system, or allow yourself to do a weak qualifying step. Almost every single time, after the crash, the investigation will reveal the deadly "pilot" error.

Nowadays, it seems that the committee decision group is more the rule than the exception. When you qualify the Commitment step and you learn that a committee will be making the decision, it is essential that you understand what process the committee is going to use to reach their decision. I was talking with the Chairman of the Board of a large insurance company. I was able to uncover plenty of pain, and determined that money was no problem for the type of sales training we were talking about. When I began qualifying the Commitment step I began it as I always do: "Jack who will be involved in making this decision"? He said "that will be our committee, Howard, there are nine of us." I responded, "Fine I will need everyone there at the presentation next week, and by the way, what process will use to come to a decision"? Jack said "Consensus." I said "you mean everyone must agree?" Dick responded "yes, that's how we always do it." I said "okay then I will give each person a 3x5 card and ask them to put their name and indicate yes or no regarding their individual commitment to the sales training program and if we don't get all yeses, we won't do the program." Dick readily agreed. A week later, after concluding the presentation to the nine board members, I collected their decision cards and asked the boss if we could go into his office and look at them together. We sat down in some comfy leather chairs around his mahogany oval conference table and I began reading the cards out loud. "Yes, yes, yes, yes, yes, yes, no, no, no -" We had six yes and three nos. I looked at Dick and said "Well I guess the program's not going to happen since we don't' have a consensus." Dick said "Howard give me the three no cards." I passed them over. Dick picked up the first one, took his pen, crossed out the No and wrote Yes, and then repeated that with the other two cards. Then he looked at me and said "there are certain privileges that go with being the Chairman. When can we get started?" I learned a few things from that experience. First, when dealing with a committee, make sure the power is on your side. Second, using the individual ballot method turns the committee decision into a series of individual decisions, which are much easier to change (by whatever method), and third, make sure you discuss the ballots with the boss in private.

I can also remember a sales call that didn't go so well. During the commitment step I asked Dan, my contact, if he would be the one making the decision. He answered yes. When I showed up for the solution presentation I was greeted by six people sitting at a large conference table and they were introduced to me as managers of individual departments. Dan said, "Since these folks run the departments that will impacted by the training, I thought they should weigh in on the decision." That was when I made my mistake. I went right ahead and gave the presentation I had prepared for Dan to the group. At the end I heard, "Why do we need this kind of training Dan?", "How much is it going to cost my department"?, etc. What happened is the *group* was not qualified and the sale blew up right in my face. What I should have done was press Dan on his decision making process instead of just accepting his yes answer. It's not uncommon for a manager or boss to want to say (and believe) he is the decision maker, and they don't generally volunteer that they seek input from staff or colleagues. But with a few additional questions, this information can usually be uncovered.

If I had asked follow up questions, here's how the conversation would likely have gone:

Me: Dan, what type of decision making process do you usually go through?

Dan: Well, I make the final decision, but sometimes I'll get some opinions from other people.

Me: That makes sense. In this specific situation, do you think you'll be seeking any input?

Dan: I'll probably want to include the heads of the departments that will receive the training. *Me*: Great. How many departments would that be?

Dan: It will be 6 departments.

Me: And how will you solicit their opinions? Will you have a meeting? Send an email…?

Dan: Well, I suppose I'll have them sit in on our next meeting and then they can hear from you what the training program will be like.

Me: Ok. Well Dan, my concern with that is that you and I have been talking for a while now and we've already worked out a few things and I'm worried that if the rest of the group comes in late to the conversation, they might not be able to make informed decisions. What would you think about me meeting with them before the solution presentation, and then we can make sure that everyone is on the same page, and everyone is able to make a fully informed decision when we get to that point?

Dan: I guess that makes sense. I'll set it up.

So, from here I would sit down with the entire group, and start to quality the whole group for pain and money and then start from commitment with the entire group and go forward from there, ending with a secret ballot at the end of the presentation.

The rule that gets enacted with this example is to always be sure **all** the decision makers are on the same page with the Pain and the Money **before** you close.

The other lesson from this example is that when I showed up to do the presentation and was surprised by the additional people, I should have stopped and aborted the solution presentation. Ideally I would have been able to convince Dan to let me talk to the other decision makers and qualify them, but if not then it's still better to abort the mission than to plow ahead and lose the sale.

Closing

Closing is the least important part of the system we have been discussing and the reason is that if you're presenting a solution to a person who has the problem you can fix, has the money to pay for the solution, and is the one making the decision to spend the money to fix the problem, then your sale is 80% closed (assuming you do have the solution). The emphasis is on the qualifying steps, not on the close.

The simplest way to describe what to do in the closing step is to say "Do whatever it takes to help the prospect see and believe that you have the solution to his or her pain". That can take many forms: power point, written proposal, conversation etc. The rules of the presentation itself are simple. Start by reviewing all the pains that you uncovered in the Pain step. Make sure that you gain agreement from the prospect that his pains still exist and see if there are any new ones to add. Then review your agreement on the Money and Commitment steps. Finally remind the prospect of the yes or no decision agreement following the presentation. The review of the previous agreements is an essential and powerful part of the closing process because you never know what might have changed in the prospect's mind, world, or heart between your last meeting and your closing meeting.

I can remember a time when I had qualified the two partners in a trucking business through Pain, Money and Commitment, and then showed up for the scheduled Closing Presentation meeting. I was up at the white board, marker in hand, and the two partners were seated in front of me as I began my review. I listed all the Pains we had discussed at the last qualifying meeting and they all agreed with them.

Next I reviewed our agreement on budget and I sensed their body language communicating discomfort. I stopped and asked if there was a problem with the money. They proceeded to tell me that they'd been thinking about the amount of money they would be spending with me and they had started to feel that there were other things they could be spending that money on. I asked them to tell me what those things were and I proceeded to list them on the board.

When the list was complete I began with the first item which was office furniture and asked them what kind of ROI they had hoped to get by investing money in office furniture. We went down the list and last was the sales training I was selling. It became clear that sales training by far had the largest ROI of anything else on the list. They recommitted to spending the money if they liked what they saw in my presentation and their body language relaxed. With that hurdle now cleared, we reviewed the yes/no decision agreement and I moved on to a successful close.

Never underestimate the power of the review. If I hadn't done it you know what would have happened: the end would have come and I would have gotten a maybe or a NO if I was strong enough to hold them to the decision agreement. It may have been possible to learn about the money problem after the presentation but you will find that you have more power to eliminate the objections and concerns **before** you show them how you will fix the pain. The prospect is simply more cooperative when they are in pain and anticipating the fix.

If everything checks out on the review you are ready to go for the presentation. Begin by addressing the pains one at a time and applying your solution. After you address a specific pain ask the prospect for their okay before proceeding to the next one. This ensures that you've addressed every question and nuance of how your solution will solve the pain in the client's mind. Again, never assume you know what the client's thinking. After all the pains are addressed it's time to collect your decision.

Remember: don't be afraid of the no. It is **always** better than the maybe. The truth is that if you have done the qualifying hard and well, your closing ratio will be very high. Any sale that doesn't close should be debriefed by working backward through the steps of the system to see where you weakened so you can strengthen it for the next sale. That is how you get stronger and stronger.

THE PHILOSOPHY AND PSYCHOLOGY OF THE SELLING SYSTEM

Now that you understand the steps, you need to learn the philosophy and psychology behind the system.

Person not the Product

There is a traditional method of selling that emphasizes the features and benefits of a product in order to sell it. This premise worked after the industrial revolution for many years but doesn't work today because there are so many duplications of similar products. This phenomenon has been referred to as the "commoditization of America" or the "commodity selling paradigm" model – where every product gets cheaper and it gets harder to differentiate one product from another. For a period of time following the industrial revolution new and unique products were being manufactured all the time. These one of kind items like the mouse trap or dishwasher, TV, radio etc. were all new and unique. When the first Macintosh computer with 128K of memory was invented and was, pretty much, the only personal computing option available I, along with millions of other excited people, went out and bought one for $3000. Now, a wide variety of PC's exist, including desk tops with way more power and ability that can be had for $300. That is the deflation commodity spiral that I am referring to. An example in the service industry is the prospect who owns a business and is thinking of doing some radio advertising. He calls the five radio stations in his market for a pitch. They all tell him that they are number one in the market and they each have a carefully crafted presentation to prove that. The prospect ends up confused, thinking "how can they all be number one? Someone must be lying." The sell more easily selling system is designed to make it easy for the salesperson to differentiate themselves, within this commodity environment, by focusing on the pain of the prospect and customizing the solution to fit the specific situation that the prospect is in.

I believe that the commodity paradigm does accurately reflect the problem that traditional selling methods face. A newer approach based, on an awareness of the commodity perception is the

Pain/Solution Model

Pain/Solution Selling basically states that people have problems that cause them pain and they need products and services to take the pain away in the form of a solution. According to the solution model, it doesn't make much sense to pitch features and benefits before conducting an in depth interview with the prospect and identifying and understanding the nature of the problem, as the person perceives it and what the best fit for a product/service solution might be. It's important to remember that people buy for their reasons, not ours. For pain to be real it must meet three criteria, it must be personal, specific and emotional. An example in the insurance business is when the prospect has a claim and they are upset because they cannot get their insurance agent to call them back. Something this simple meets all three criterions: Personal – I am not being helped, Specific – there is a hole in my roof and, emotional – I am very frustrated and upset about it. If an insurance agent happens to cold call this person at this time they will have no trouble developing the pain step.

Embracing this idea of pain has many ramifications when translated into selling behavior. The traditional feature/benefit model has the salesman doing most of the talking, explaining, presenting. The Pain/solution model put's the salesperson in more of an interviewer mode, asking questions and listening. The assumption here is that the person knows best what problems, challenges they are facing and what the best way to fix it would be. The salesperson's interview then is for the purpose of uncovering the pain and helping the prospect to paint their picture of what the perfect solution would look, feel, sound, and taste like, and then attempt to sell their picture back to them. It follows then that every solution would be tailored and customized for the specific set of issues that the prospect is presenting. This perception of tailored, customized solutions is the ultimate method of destroying the commodity concept. The age of commodity must inevitably be replaced by the age of customization if today's companies are to continue to reap high margins while differentiating themselves in an increasingly competitive marketplace.

For the salesperson, the focus then shifts from the product to the person. Relationship management becomes the primary focus rather than an excellent product presentation. The focus for salespeople learning and using this selling system must now be on building relationship communication skills such as: asking questions, listening, nurturing, establishing rapport early, etc. Skills that ultimately help the salesperson to understand what his prospect/customer is up against and then help the prospect to see how the salesperson's product/service is in fact a good fit to take away the pain.

Psychology Behind The Selling System

Since in my former life I was a professor of psychology, I have applied basic principles of human behavior to my selling system, and believe these are principals that every salesperson needs to know in order to effectively work this selling system. If you read the book, I'm Ok, You're Ok by Thomas Harris, (it was very popular in the 70's) then you know the basic structure of the theory. Harris postulated a theory he called Transactional Analysis, in which he maintained that people communicated with each other from three basic ego states he labeled Parent, Adult and Child (PAC).

Parent (P)

The Parent ego state is pretty well developed by the time one is six years old. To understand what the parent ego state is, picture a new born baby with a digital recorder in its brain. The recorder turns on when he is born and stays on twenty –four hours a day, recording the messages that are fed into it. In the first six years of life, we are usually hanging around with our parents and all the talking they do to us goes on that recorder to be played back anytime somebody says something that pushes the play button. All this communicated information is stored unconsciously so the material is uncensored and unedited. The content consists of prejudice and opinion. So, right from the beginning, we internalize a package of pre-set ways of looking at the world, kind of a brain transplant from our parents' opinions about just about everything. This is the Parent ego state. The parent messages are largely either critical or nurturing.

In the Sell More Easily System certain words are what we call "parent" words. These words are helpful cues that tell us when the person we are talking to is being influenced by early, recorded, opinions or prejudices. The Critical Parent frequently uses the words, "Don't, Do, Not, No, Always, Never, Good, Bad, Right, Wrong, Should and Must." The word "Be" is a significant "Parent" word too, because it transforms into "behave, be nice, be rich, be smart". The word "You," is often used in front of these words and phrases by the critical parent ego state. "You should always. You must never. You had better not." So, the "Critical Parent," we will describe as, the opinionated, prejudicial, part of people's behavior. And note, when I say "prejudicial", I only mean that this is the pre-judgment part where attitudes and ideas about people, yourself, money, time, what to worry about, what is and what is not important, come from.

For example: "John, my daughter is planning on marrying a salesman." The taped Parent opinion response might be "Oh, that's too bad. Salesmen are always in debt".

The word *always* is a typical Parent word and provides the clue to the Parent statement. The parent is where the prospects objections and stalls come from. Critical parenting is not very useful for our business. A nurturing parent is very kind, very helpful, supportive and, consulting,. In sales, we are going to come toward the prospect from, usually, a nurturing point of view, and we call that "Assertiveness" rather than from the aggressiveness of the critical parent.

Adult (A)

The Adult ego state can be likened to "the computer" of the personality because it is always analytical, rational and logical. The Adult ego state is the great fact finder and operates without the influence of the parent.

The words that identify this ego state are "who, what, where, when, why, and how." Any time you are asking for information, asking a question, you are operating out of this computer, this data bank. You are as objective as you are going to be. As a matter of fact, if you were purely in the adult state without any contamination from the other two, you would be like Spock on Star Trek. You would be constantly rational and analytical. Also, rather boring at times. So when you are doing a fact finding sales interview and asking lots of questions and keeping your assumptions to a minimum your Adult ego state is in charge.

Child (C)

The third ego state is the Child. The Child ego state is where emotions live. The primary emotions being, for our purposes: Mad, Glad, Sad, and Scared. When you are experiencing any of these emotions your Child ego state is in control of your personality. There are also words that identify when someone you are talking to has been taken over by their Child ego state. The most important word cue to identify the Child ego state is the word "I." This is the "I, Me, Mine," part of behavior. You will hear phrases such as "I like, I hope, I wish, I want." And that helps you identify the child ego state.

If you are experiencing any one of those feelings, you are in your child ego state. You can only be in one at a time, but you can move rapidly from one to the other.

The rule in my selling system is that "People buy emotionally" so it is good to recognize when your prospect is in the Child ego state. Later, when I talk about sure fire questions to read out the emotional state of your prospect you will understand why one of the questions I may suggest is "What are you hoping I can do for you?"

The Child is really where a lot of the action is. We talk about buying being emotional, we know how powerful emotional forces are within behavior. The child ego state can be thought of as having three parts. The first part is the "natural, or free, child", the second is the "adapted" and the third is the "rebel". Most creative and innovative ideas come from the child ego state. When you are in a sales call it is good to "get loose," because then creative ideas are likely. That is that natural, free stuff. But, this is where the adapted child steps in. We learn things as we are growing up. As we grow up we learn to be nice, to be polite, and to say please and thank you. We learn not to hurt people's feelings and, to seek approval. We learn that it's very important that people "like us. This can present a problem. You are in front of a prospect, and the natural, free part of you says "go for the kill. What are you waiting for? Just put a little pressure on the prospect. This prospect has to have pressure – not every prospect, but *this* one does." So you start to put on the pressure, and you see the person react. You probably have been there – you know, the tie opens up, the knees are going 45 RPM's and he looks at his watch a couple of times and all of a sudden, you say "Sir, it looks like you're having a hard time making a decision." "You bet I am." "Look, here's my card. Give me a call." You leave. Usually you let the pressure off just one moment or two before he's about to say, "Okay, let's do it." When you let the pressure off, what is happening? Why are you letting it off? What in you is motivating your behavior? "Be nice. Be nice. Be nice; and don't put people under pressure and don't make people mad at you."

For your whole life, you have been trained to be nice and to be polite. Then you end up in a sales company, and the manager gets in front of the salespeople and he says "Okay folks, remember, you've got to KILL to SELL. Now go out there and go for the jugular." How do you reverse years of training like that? It's very, very, hard. I have a rule. The rule says: "There are no social calls in sales. When it starts feeling good, there is probably something going wrong your Adapted Child is running the show.

The Rebel child is the third part of the child ego state, and is the part that does the opposite of what your parents said to do. "Don't do this," to the rebel means "Do"; and, "Do this" means" Don't". That's why critical parent does not work well. If I say to the prospect, "I can't believe you are doing that," he will react with "you are damn right I'm doing that. Who are you to tell me?!" Instead, reverse psychology is needed." It's almost like Judo, because you use the momentum of the other person to defeat them. In sales it might sound like this "The suit looks great on you Mr. Prospect but the price might be out of your budget" or "many people are buying and loving this car, but you may want something more conservative Mrs. Bloom." These examples are examples of selling to the rebel child or as we sometimes call it "negative selling." In essence it is good old fashioned reverse psychology.

Communication and Transactional Analysis

So, these are the three ego states: opinionated, pre-judgmental parent; factual, analytical adult; emotional and feeling child. Research shows that when two people communicate, the chances that they will both be in their adult ego state, and are grounded in the same reality, probably happens 15% of the time. In sales, it is probably more like 5% of the time. Most of the time, when you are talking with someone, you will find that ego states are jumping around. Once you are aware of it, it almost becomes fun to start picking them out as they appear.

There are three types of communication, or transactions that we are going to look at. A transaction is defined as a communication unit, which is composed of a stimulus and a response. You say "Hi, how are you," I say "Fine." Stimulus, response, we just had a transaction. The three types of transactions we're going to look at are Complimentary, Cross, and Ulterior.

Complimentary Transactions.

A matched transaction, adult to adult for example, is called a "complimentary transaction" not because of the content, but because of where the transaction starts and finishes.

Complimentary transactions are a great way to begin building rapport with your prospect, because everyone generally stays OK during complimentary transactions. For example, we're talking about sports – you love the Yankees, I love the Yankees. You're in parent and I'm in parent. You have opinions and I have opinions and we are sharing them with each other.

An example of a complimentary Adult to Adult transaction would be, you ask me how to get to downtown Chicago, and I give you directions. An example of complimentary Child to Child transaction would be, we're at a bar, the Yankees just won and we are slapping high fives and cheering.

It is important to understand that complimentary transactions **are not necessarily positive nor are they always productive.** As a matter of fact, in a sales call, you can go too far on the complimentary, and never be able to move the sale past the opening stages. Have you ever tried to sell to a group of engineers? Those guys operate primarily out of their adult ego state and all they want is another study and another example and another ledger, and they never get excited enough to buy anything. If you only engage in complimentary transactions, you'll never move out of adult, never find pain, never tap any emotion and never close the sale.

The alternative to complimentary transactions is cross transactions, and they too can be productive or unproductive depending on their application.

Cross Transactions

Let's use Marty and his wife as an example for cross transactions. This is going to be a diagram of an argument. Husband wakes up in the morning and he's looking for his keys and he can't find them. He's ready to go to work and he says to his wife, "Where are my keys?"

Transaction #1

Marty		Wife
Parent		Parent
Adult	⟶	Adult
Child		Child

Marty starts in adult because he's
seeking information.

But his wife says "How should I know?!" Which means she's received his message in child and responded from child.

Transaction #2

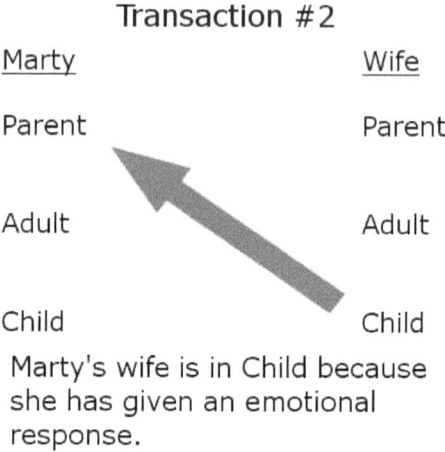

Marty   Wife

Parent   Parent

Adult   Adult

Child   Child

Marty's wife is in Child because she has given an emotional response.

BUT then the wife continues and says: "You know, if you kept your keys in the same place every day, you wouldn't have this problem, would you?"

Transaction #3

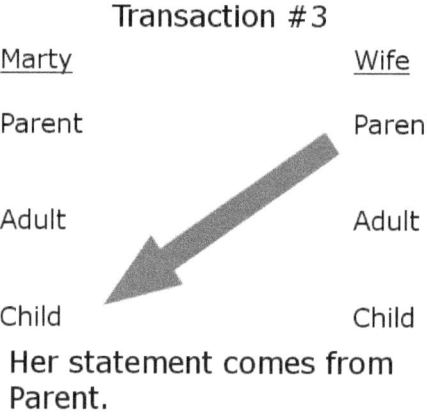

Marty   Wife

Parent   Parent

Adult   Adult

Child   Child

Her statement comes from Parent.

With a statement coming out of Parent, it can be received in child by Marty, depending on his communication history with his wife and his mood and focus in that moment.

So here's our cross: Marty started in adult, his message was received in Child and then sent back in Parent. Why did that happen? What caused the shift from "How should I know?" to "you should know,"? The best defense is a good offense. This is really critical.

In this scenario Marty chooses to say "Well maybe I'd be able to find them if you kept the house cleaner."

Transaction #4

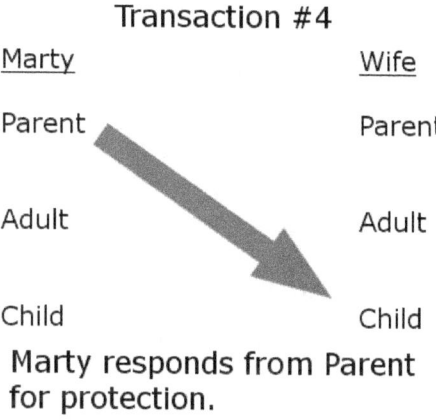

Marty responds from Parent for protection.

Even though Marty's wife receives the comment in child, she transfers it internally to her parent as a self-protection mechanism. Now, from parent she says "It's not easy keeping the house neat with a slob like you living here."

Transaction #5

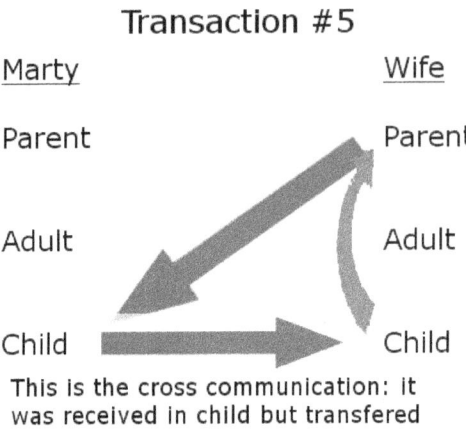

Marty   Wife

Parent   Parent

Adult   Adult

Child   Child

This is the cross communication: it was received in child but transfered to parent.

The most likely response for Marty to give will be from his parent ego state, because now he's going to be feeling attacked in his child ego state and he will go to his internal parent for help. This is a very common scenario, and it even has a name, because psychologists have to name everything. This is called the Game of Uproar. And the Game of Uproar means that, the transactions will keep getting more and more emotional as each person tries to defend themselves against the emotional attacks by attacking back. And it just ends, well, in an uproar: the dish flies and the guy ducks on his way out the door.

But we never get any compromise, or resolution, or real communication in the sense of an actual exchange of information.

What ego state is missing in this? The Adult. So let's put the Adult in here: Marty says: "Honey, I can see you are upset. Why don't we just let it drop. I'll get the keys some other way." Or, at the start of the interaction, when Marty asks where the keys are the wife can simply say "I don't know".

Transaction #4-REDO

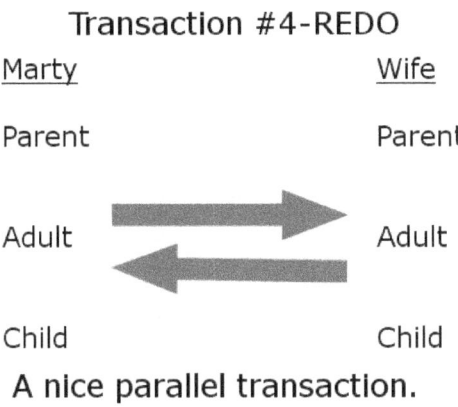

<u>Marty</u>	<u>Wife</u>
Parent	Parent
Adult	Adult
Child	Child

A nice parallel transaction.

But do you know what happens when he's about to do it? Suddenly a voice appears in his head, and its parent talking to his child saying: "You're a wimp! Are you going to take that crap from her?" And so chances are high that he's going to respond from his child and its game on again.

What I want you to see is that when someone gets upset with you - when the prospect comes at you negatively for example, probably the moment that happened or a second before that is that they got scared, or angry, and they went for protection. If we stay in our adult, we don't allow ourselves to drop down to child and get scared by that. Suddenly we can begin to make use of it.

Let me give you another way to look at it. Johnny is 9 years old and he's in the third grade. In school he gets bullied by some bigger kids. He feels very intimidated and he's scared and he goes running home and when he gets home, who is he looking for? Mom, Dad, Big Brother – for help, for protection. That's normal. He's only 9. Then Johnny grows up. He is 50 years old. But he still has little Johnny inside his personality in the form of that Child Ego State. This time he gets intimidated by a client, by a prospect. He gets that same scared feeling that he got when he was 9, except he feels funny calling his mom for help now. She is 90 has a cane and he doesn't get the same security feeling. So now he has learned to internalize that protection in the form of a parent ego state. It's like a knee jerk response – when that little guy inside him gets scared, he goes to his internal parent and attacks the external source of his fear. The same thing happens when the husband can't find his car keys and his wife berates him for being careless. He feels attacked in "Child" and responds from parent and says, "Hey, maybe I could find my keys if you kept the house a little straighter."

Ulterior Transaction

An ulterior transaction is one that is happening below the surface. The principals of T/A still apply, these ulterior transactions will still be between your different ego states, but they will be running underneath the actual, surface transactions. Which is a fancy, academic way of saying that this is an analysis of lying. The psychological definition of lying: when someone is saying one thing but they mean something else. Sometimes they know they're lying, and sometimes they don't. When it comes to sales, here's the rule with regard to lying: if you feel like someone is lying to you –they are. In other words, the "ulterior communication" is that there is an undercurrent that conflicts with what they are actually saying.

When you use an indirect question, you get a direct answer. What it means is that people lie to you if you ask them directly, as in "Where are you going tonight?" You are putting them in a position where it's going to be more of an opportunity for them to lie because they are feeling "pinned." But if you say, "You don't want to tell me where you're going, do you?" that's more of an indirect question. Using reverse psychology is easier for them to tell the truth. So they will say, "Well, sure, I'm going out to X".

When you get that feeling in your gut that there is an ulterior transaction happening, you'll be right 95% of the time. This is because in the child ego state there is a little professor that operates on hunch and intuition, and is the built-in "BS Detector". When you started out in life, you didn't know the language. How did you get around? You felt it. You felt everything, and your feelings are 95% correct. All we have to do is to re-learn to trust them. So when you get a feeling that someone is lying to you, I want you to call it. "Calling it" means you try to surface the lie. But it's not easy. It will take some probing, sometimes several attempts to unearth the information contained within the ulterior transaction.

Ulterior transactions can be difficult to spot because they come in all shapes and sizes.

Example #1

Your prospect goes off on you very negatively: "Your product is way too expensive. I am not at all interested, and I don't need it, so please leave" If the salesperson stays in his adult ego state and analyzes the prospect's reaction as a Critical Parent protective response, then this would be what the salesperson hears as the ulterior message "please stop selling because I will buy it, you see I want it and need it but am afraid to spend the money and get yelled at by my parent." Whether this is true or not is not so important because if the salesperson hears it that way he is much more likely to respond with something adult like "no problem, I am sure it is not right for you to have this and I will leave immediately, but could I ask you one more question first?" The prospect is now feeling released and relieved generally responds "sure". Our professionally trained salesperson says " I sensed that you did like the product when I demonstrated how it worked, so I guess it was something I said or did that made you angry with me." Assuming there was real interest detected by the salesperson early on, the usual response to this set of moves would be "Well, that's true. I did like it but I got nervous about the money" . So now the real truth comes forward and the prospect, non-defensively from child, begins to share real feelings and the sale can proceed to a likely positive outcome. In essence when the salesperson is the psychiatrist total objectivity regarding the prospect's responses is achieved and the most appropriate responses to get the truth of the situation will be spoken.

Example #2:

This is a Salesperson to Prospect ulterior transaction. You've sent the guy a proposal. You call the guy up and say:

Salesperson: Did you get the proposal?

Prospect: Yes.

S: How do you like it?

P: I like it fine.

S: That's great! Then I'll expect a check on the date indicated so we can get started.

P: There are just a couple of things we've got to do; we'll get back to you.

Now, you might say to yourself, "well that is an adult statement, because this guy probably really means what he is saying." However, there is likely something deep inside you that is saying something else, and what you're feeling is, the prospect was really saying, "We're not committed to sending the check and we don't want to tell you why."

Prospect: We're not ready to send the check yet.

Salesperson: I get the feeling there is a problem.

P: There's no problem. We like you.

S: I appreciate that, but I felt like you're hesitating on sending the check--was that just me?

P: Well no, that has nothing to do with whether we like it or not; it's our third partner.

S: Third partner?

P: Yeah, he wants to look at it

S: Well, what if he doesn't like it?

P: oh, he'll like it. He does whatever we say.

S: I'm a lottery player, one out of a million he doesn't like it. Then what?

P: Well then, we can't do it.

S: well, maybe I should be at that meeting when he looks it

P: well, ok.

What we have is the prospect giving a veiled threat to you from their parent to your child "Don't push. If you push, you may lose it all." And you know, we have another rule which says, "you can't lose what you don't have." It's very important to remind yourself of this rule, because that feeds your adult. When you look at it with your adult, you've got nothing. When you look at it with your child, "Oh, I may have something." And the child tends to make it bigger and bigger, and once your child gets into the sales call, you are about to blow it because you'll think you have it and you'll start overlooking details. So leave your child in the car when you go on sales calls. Crack the window a little, if it's a hot day though.

Ok/Not Ok

When I left teaching I was warned by many of my colleagues that I should simply get another teaching job and that if I didn't I would surely get chewed up "out there." "Out there" is how cloistered institutional workers like teachers in a college refer to the normal "work a day" world that most of us inhabit. In the early days of my selling experience there were many times I was inclined to agree with those naysayers and to wonder if I had what it took to survive, in the jungle. Since I had spent so many years in the education system, I used the metaphor I was most familiar with and began to refer to the environment I was traveling in as *Screw University*, Screw U for short. There are many professors in Screw U and I had my share, but of course they all taught me something. Like the food broker in Syracuse, New York I cold called one day. Tony, the owner, listened to my opening and looked at me, then said "do you want to write a big order today?" I replied "I would absolutely love to!" This was my 25th call with no results. Tony clearly sensed my eagerness and told me he would be right back, and with that he got up walked to the back of his store and disappeared through a door. I sat as the suspense grew and calculated in my head the amount of money Tony would spend with me and how proud and happy my wife and kids were going to be when I finally came home with a large check. The suspense was palpable. Then the door finally opened and Tony emerged with one of those 3 foot gag pens, and a shit eating grin on his face. He handed it to me and said "Now you can write a really big order with this pen." But clearly he meant somewhere else, because all I was getting there was an humiliating lesson.

Let's analyze the food broker's behavior in terms of the OK/not OK theory. The rule is, people feel ok about themselves by finding other people that are more not ok than they are. If we look at the world through Tony's eyes here is what we might see. Tony gets up in the morning and gets yelled at by his wife because he forgot to pick up the prescription at the drugstore the night before. He looks in the mirror and laments the fatty desert he ate at midnight. Tony gets into work and a good customer rags him out about an order that was screwed up. Tony is feeling very not ok and so he has to make someone else not okay in order for him to feel okay again. The someone else has to be a neutral, non-threatening target, unlike a wife or a customer. And who better than a…wait what do I see in the distance? Is it? Why, yes it is, it's a salesman coming to call on me and what's more it's a young, new salesman- perfect target! Tony instinctively knows he can easily make this sales guy not ok and get back his own okay-ness with no problem. Which is exactly what he did to me.

That scenario is played out day after day and it is one of the things that makes the sales profession so demanding. The official psychological theory is called "Displaced Aggression" which is when someone makes you feel bad, but you believe you have too much to lose if you retaliated, so you look for a less threatening target and let them have it with both barrels. Did you ever get an unexpected attack from someone you were harmlessly asking a favor of, and suddenly you got a whole lot more aggression than seemed appropriate for the situation? Well, what likely happened was that you fell victim to somebody who had just been ragged out by their boss and they had both cannons loaded just as little old you appeared. When the salesperson making the call looks and acts needy it is like printing on your forehead the words "I am so not okay, get your okay needs met here", and they will, you can be sure.

Understanding the psychology behind the ok/not okay behavior is what saved me from quitting sales entirely. First I had to work on myself and eliminate all my neediness and not okay behavior when calling on a prospect. Second I had to recognize that when my prospect seemed to behave aggressively toward me or even passive-aggressively that they were displaying not ok behavior which meant that they were hurting. The next, and arguably most important step is to apply the remedy, which is to build up the prospect's self-esteem with compliments and the other techniques you will learn in this book.

The main lesson is don't get sucked into the game; stay objective, use the qualifying system I'm teaching you, and maintain control, of your own emotions, if nothing else.

Never assume you won't have to deal with the ok/not ok theory on a sales call. There can be a temptation, in an attempt at self-preservation, to think things like "well these are executives, they'll be fair," or "well these are [fill in industry], they won't try to make me feel bad." And the moment you start thinking like that, is the moment you'll get smacked with a not ok lesson so hard, you'll see stars.

This is exactly what happened to me when I met with three insurance agency leaders who wanted to discuss sales training for their combined sales force of over 40 sales people. I qualified them through the three steps of the Boss Talk and proceeded to set up the solution presentation. When I arrived the three men were seated in the conference room and I proceeded to set up my easel and markers.

I began my presentation and probably wasn't more than 8 minutes into it when one of the men stood up and said "Don't mind me Howard, I am listening" as he walked over to his large credenza in the corner of the room and extracted a basket with shoe shining supplies in it. He sat down, pulled out his chair so he could more easily reach his shoes to apply polish and looked up at me and once again assured me that he was listening. Well I continued to present and by the time I was done, about 30 minutes later, all three men had very well shined shoes and I had no sale. To say I felt not okay from this experience, is putting it way too mildly. Saying I felt like a lower life form might be more accurate.

I immediately called Ed my partner and mentor at the time and asked him what he would have done. In characteristic Ed fashion he said "I would have stopped presenting, sat down and said what a good idea, pass the polish". Oh how I'd wished I would have done that. Again I had so much positive expectation wrapped up in this deal my deflation paralyzed my ability to respond in any meaningful way instead of "I'll get back to you".

Another lesson learned and it is a derivative of the last one **Never let your neediness show, Kill all your expectations of an end result.** Expectations make you vulnerable to neediness when it looks like you won't get what you so badly wish and hope for, then you end up wimping out and paralyzing all your power.

I guess I learned a thing or two because as you'll see in this next story, I consciously leveraged not okay behavior into maximum rapport and best of all, a sale.

There was the top guy who ran the very large Trust department in a well-known bank and here is how this meeting went. I arrived at the 35th floor of a beautiful high rise building in metro NY. Sam opened his office door and cordially invited me to sit down at his mahogany round conference table. The office impressed me, all windows looking out at the city, the office was probably a little smaller than my house at the time. Sam looked at me and said "Howard do you have a card?" "No sir not with me." Now the body language of this dude was, arms folded, legs crossed, 2000 dollar suit with diamond stick pin in a $500 silk tie. Remember I believe in the naked sales call, bring nothing and allow yourself to be perceived as not okay to gain control of the prospect.

Well, Sam gives me a funny look, but it gets worse, because he was talking in a very intellectual manner. I stopped him and said "you are saying something really important Sam, and I sure would like to write it down." As I said this I checked both pockets for a pen which of course were empty on purpose. Sam looked at me with a look that was a combination of a scowl and a suddenly very bad smell he was experiencing. Then he got up and walked over to his giant mahogany credenza opened the doors, took something off the shelf, walked back to the table, sat down re-crossed his arms and legs and with a very agile flick of his wrist he slid something over to me. It was a leather bound note pad and when I opened it I saw a gold cross pen, a small gold calculator and a glow in the dark hot stamped linen business card. This was obviously what Sam gave out to his wealthy clients. He must have seen the look of astonishment on my face because generally when I made that move I got a plain yellow legal pad and a Bick pen. Sam with eyes downcast said "keep it", and that was the breaking point from the standpoint of the ok/not ok psychology. After his scowling, upturned nose, downcast eyes and crossed everything "keep it," he uncrossed everything, opened his tie, unbuttoned the top button of his shirt leaned back in his chair and smiled broadly. He then said "Howard I learned how to sell in my father's shoe store when I was five years old......." He talked for about 30 minutes - rapport, pain, all of it and then signed a training contract for his staff of 30 people.

So there you have it, acting not okay on purpose can put big dollars in your pocket.

Let's review the two ok/not ok rules: 1. People feel okay by finding other people that are more not okay than they are and 2. As a professional salesperson your job is to make sure the prospect is feeling okay about themselves *all the time*. In order to execute rule number two you sometimes have to act not ok on purpose and let your prospect feel all kinds of superior to you. When that happens the prospect feels secure and comfortable and it is easier for you to gain rapport and get the honest information you need to properly qualify the prospect.

At the end of the day, what matters is making the sale, not feeling superior to your prospect.

Self-Limiting Beliefs

In the old days of sales training, prospecting was about making the cold calls which meant knocking on office doors all day. Rejection came standard and it was starting to get to me. Until John, an old sales training coach who I met at a seminar, helped me to open my mind and it made all the difference.

One rainy afternoon I sat in a coffee shop with John and poured my heart out to him about how bad I was feeling about all the rejection I was getting; how I felt like nobody in the whole world wanted to talk to me and I felt like jumping off a roof I was so frustrated. John asked me one simple question that I will never forget, he said "Howard when you are going into make a cold call, what is it that you're thinking about, what are you visualizing?" I told him that I was thinking about some mean executive who doesn't want to waste his time listening to some doofus talk about sales training.

"Howard," he said, "that is your problem". He went on to say that when he was out selling and making cold calls, on the way to the call he would picture the following: a large banner would be hanging out in front of the office door and it would say "Welcome John!", then a red carpet would come rolling out of door with five trumpeters in parade dress uniform announcing in melodious tones the arrival of me, *The Salesman*. "Howard," he went on, "by the time I was sitting in front of the boss I felt important and I believed the boss appreciated me and realized that he was very lucky to have me there to help him grow his business".

That was my first big lesson on how as Hamlet said: "nothing either good or bad but thinking makes it so". Your thoughts are a symptom of what you believe and beliefs can be either helpful or self-limiting success killers. The lesson I got from John stayed with me. I was able to rid myself of the negative head trash and form a positive belief system around cold calling which manifested itself in positive thoughts and visualizations that made all the difference. So if you dread prospecting whether by phone or in person, check the baggage you're carrying. Have a serious talk with yourself and learn about the thoughts, visualizations and beliefs that you may need to trash and replace, then watch what happens to your bank account.

Self-Limiting Beliefs and Money Concepts

One of my clients was in the computer reselling business before computers were everywhere and the prices came down. At one of the sales meetings the discussion centered around a computer part that was in demand and all of the six salespeople had each sold one to one of their customers. I thought this would be an excellent opportunity to ask each salesperson what they sold the part for. Three people sold it for $500 two for $300 and one for $2500. Not surprisingly the top performer in the group sold it for $2500, the lowest performer in the group sold for only $300.   After all the numbers were revealed the low guy looks at the top guy and says "$2500?! You can't sell it for that!" and the top guy answers "No, YOU can't."

What did the top guy mean when he said that? He meant that the only variable between them was an internal belief system with regard to what their product and services were worth. Self-limiting beliefs are the most destructive when it comes to your money concept.

Remember we talked about the HPP earlier? Well what the research also shows us is that most of the time what the salesperson conceives of as the maximum price the prospect will pay is lower that what the prospect will actually pay. *This means that most salespeople will leave money on the table as a result of their internal belief system about money.* John called this phenomenon "Selling out of your Pocket". This is what happens when a salesperson judges what his customer will spend based on the projection of his own belief system about money. The salesperson's belief is based on what **he** would spend and he projects it into the mind of his prospect. So if a sales person is frugal, if he's someone who always hunts for a bargain in his personal life, who expects to be able to haggle with every salesperson he encounters, then he will not only accept it when a prospect does that to him, but he will actually expect it. Conversely, if a salesperson respects a sales associate's time, recognizes that you have to pay for quality, and generally doesn't require that he always find the cheapest option when shopping for himself, then he expects the same from a prospect and will not tolerate a bargain hunter. In the above story about the computer sales people, what do you think the salesperson who sold the part for $2500 believed?

A few years ago I had a prospect fully qualified through the pain and money step but when we got to the commitment step he told me he couldn't make the decision without his partner who was the money guy. So we set up another meeting with both partners for the presentation. We gathered in the conference room and I began the review. "Joe and I have agreed that these are the sales problems you need to fix and we agreed on $12,000 for the fee to fix them. Tim, are you on board with that so far?" Well, I could see right away why Tim was the money man because he had the kind of too serious poker face that made Clint Eastwood look relaxed. After sitting in silence for about three minutes he finally says "And I am sure that number is negotiable Howard, correct?" Now he puts this total dead expressionless stare into my inner soul that shook me and put me on the horns of the "walk your talk" dilemma that comes in many shapes and forms.

Well, I wanted this deal *bad,* but he's looking at me in such a way that it seems clear that if I don't lower the price we have no deal and I'm going to go hungry.

But, one of the pains these guys had was that their salespeople weren't holding margins because they were lowering the price and giving discounts too easily – basically his salespeople had low money concepts. I thought to myself, "Why would he hire a person to fix that problem who engages in the same behavior?"

When I looked at it like that, it was clear that I really had no choice. I straightened up my backbone, reminded myself of the value of my time and services to find enough courage and said "No the price is the price that we already agreed to and it is not negotiable. Does that mean it's over?" Now here comes the real lesson in all this: He continues to stare at me through eyes like ice for about two more minutes (although it felt like closer to an hour) and then he breaks out into this huge ear to ear grin and says "Can't blame me for trying!" and the deal went down for the 12K.

Later he told me that the moves he made on me he always makes on sales people when it comes down to the money and most of the time he gets them to discount on average 20%. Money negotiation is always a game and the rule is that in sales you get as much money as you believe you should get. Any prospect that has read one business book has read about making moves with the money to get discounts. Remember *it is a game.* Don't get hooked and emotionally involved in the game. Know and believe in the worth of your product and don't ever, ever, EVER lower your price. Now that doesn't mean if affordability is truly the issue that you can't change your offering to fit the prospect's budget. It means that once you set a price that you believe is fair for a specific service or product that you stick to it and not allow yourself to be vulnerable to the money games most prospects will try to play.

In general any assumptions we carry around can become filters that act as self-limiting beliefs and will end up costing us money in sales. During a seminar I was conducting recently, a salesperson made the remark that "young people are price shoppers; they are the ones that look at consumer reports and are always looking for a bargain." You have probably already guessed that this salesperson's closing ratio was a lot better with people above a certain age. I acquainted him with the concept of self-limiting beliefs and how his belief that young people are harder to sell will limit his success with them. He has dropped the head trash and now closes all ages with no problem. So check your baggage at the door before you make the call, and watch your money grow!

GOALS AND MOTIVATION IN THE SELLING PROFESSION

Push – Pull Motivation

Selling is a tough business. A push-pull motivation system is required. The push is what pushes you out of bed in the morning. Usually, this is all of the fixed expenses in the form of material things you own, and the bills you have to pay each month.

Payments and fixed costs might be enough to push you out of bed and out the door to your first sales call, but they may not be enough to push you into that tenth sales call at four o'clock in the afternoon. This is where the pull motivation comes in. Pull motivation is about the future vision of your tangible goals-- material things that you want but don't yet have.

Our sales assessment testing of over five hundred thousand salespeople found that the most successful salespeople are those who have their own personal, visualized goals. We are talking houses, cars, vacations, etc. The juicy material "stuff" that our great economy runs on.

Visualized goals will create the pull that you need to make that second and third effort to close a sale or make that extra call. If you are reading this and realize you don't have something that gets you super excited when you think of it, find that "something" now! If it's a car, then go down and test drive the one you want and pick up a brochure. Get the price, write it on the brochure, and then put it where you will see it every day.

Work the money requirement into your goals, and plan on seeing yourself driving it within twelve months. You will experience the magic! Make sure your goal is very personal-- for you only.

Remember, this goal needs to be a selfish one that is above and beyond your fixed expenses. Fixed expenses can include other things, like college for your kids or jewelry for your wife. It's great to make other people happy, but that won't fulfill your pull requirement because the goal has to be something that turns you on and gets you excited. Salespeople who have powerful, visualized personal goals always exceed their company sales quotas.

Principle:

Start with the amount of money you want to make, and then break it down to the smallest unit of identifiable behavior that is 100 percent under your control.

9 step formula for successful prospecting management:

1.   Calculate your total monthly expenses for both your business and household. (Push)

2.   Calculate the additional income needed to achieve your personal goals. (Pull)

3.   Add these to calculate your monthly goal.

4.   Calculate your average income per sale.

5.   Divide your monthly goal by the average income per sale to determine how many sales are required each month to reach your goal.

6.   If the numbers are realistic, determine how many prospect conversations it takes to close a sale.

7.   Calculate the amount of activity required to get a conversation. (Dials, walk-ins, etc.)

8.   Compute the number of selling days in the month.

9.   List the total daily activity required to reach your monthly goal.

The Magic of Self -Management

That's it! Now you can move on to goal behavior.

Goal behavior is where you want to be in your sales profession. It means that you know exactly which behaviors you need to implement each and every day in order to ensure that you reach the amount of revenue from sales you're shooting for. There is an old sales manager adage that goes something like this:

When the salesperson's behavior is correct, she works for herself. When it is incorrect, she works for her boss.

Now you know how to calculate correct daily behavior based on your critical ratios and your push-pull motivation goals. You are now free to do whatever your heart desires with the remainder of your time.

Some bosses don't understand this concept, right? Well, if your boss doesn't get it and makes you slave at your desk like a salaried employee, please make sure you send them this book. You'll thank us when you see how much easier your life is because of it!

A Story

John was a sales person for an electrical wholesales company. In one of my sales seminars on push pull motivation, John confided that he wanted a boat very badly but couldn't seem to put aside the money for it. John and I sat down and worked out a goal plan based on the nine steps you just read. John now knew that in order to get the boat within the 12 months he projected that he would have to put an extra $1000 in sales into the bank. This meant that John would have to close 25 percent more sales at his average commission ratio. John put a picture of his beautiful boat on the pull out keyboard tray and whenever he was on a tough call and felt like quitting it, he would pull out the tray and look at his boat, and it would give him the extra push he needed to make the third and fourth effort to close the sale. Well, it didn't take John twelve months; he got his boat in nine. I went in to visit John one day and asked him what he was going to do for the extra pull motivation now that he had the boat he wanted.

John looked up at me and smiled as he slowly pulled out the desk tray to reveal a full color picture of a boat about twice the size of the one he owned now!

Mental Toughness and Neediness

Most salespeople do not stop to think about neediness and how it relates to mental toughness.

Eliminate your expectations, both positive and negative, as many of them as you can. You must do this because emotional needs jump on the back of expectations and weaken you. High expectations can lead to disappointment and place us in a state of emotional turmoil. Even brief periods of emotional instability can cloud the decision-making process, make it harder to listen, cause us to miss cues and clues on the sales call, and lead us away from following the effective steps of the selling system.

Don't expect. Don't assume. Follow the selling system. That is your only focus.

The serious, professional salesperson understands that he or she cannot go out into the world weak minded, spending emotional energy in the attempt to be liked, to be seen as smart, or to be considered important. A sales professional wants to be recognized as being effective and businesslike, that is all.

These are examples of weak minded selling:

- Accepting a maybe without asking for a yes or no decision.

- Agreeing to shorten the time required for a presentation.

- Agreeing to talk to someone other than the actual decision maker.

- Asking questions, then before the other party can respond, answering them yourself.

The questions pile up, one on the other. When you start answering your own questions and become excited or nervous, your behavior is screaming "needy!"

Each of these is an example of rushing—a fear-based behavior. Don't do it. Avoid asking questions that sound like you're rushing to close the deal. Don't let your selling show. Never frame questions that seek the "Yes" answer. *"Isn't this what you really want?"* There should be no rush to results. You have no control over the results. Your job is to focus on the qualifying steps of the selling system only and let the results take care of themselves.

Urgent "closing" or suggestions in that direction betray neediness and weakness on your part.

Wanting Versus Needing

Tough minded salespeople *want* the business but they don't *need* the business. They shift the focus of the sales call to the prospect and his pain. Instead of being "I" centered they are "other" centered. Sales professionals who master the skill of asking questions, who listen carefully to understand the prospect's world, and who take notes on what they're learning, have a great advantage. Asking and listening lets you control your neediness while discovering theirs.

Getting Past the Gate Keeper

My own neediness was activated on one of my toughest sales calls because of Sally the rejectionist, sorry I mean receptionist (or gate keeper as salespeople are known to say). Sally was tough, her main job was to keep sales people out and she did it quite well. The conversation was brief as I asked for Don Klasky and she firmly told me that he was out of the office then immediately asked who I was, what company I was with, and why I was calling. Hit with these three rapid fire questions within thirty seconds of starting the call and I was dumb struck. I answered all of Sally's questions honestly like the Boy Scout I was, and she promptly dismissed me with a "He is not interested" and a hang up.

Well after a few months of some sales training, a conversation with a gate keeper like Sally sounded more like this:

"Sally you have a tough job. You've got to keep guys like me out all the time." This makes her start to feel pretty good, or a little OK, and so I quickly follow up with "Put me through," in a straight parent tonality. Sally says, "Well, what's this about?" and I answer, "I'll handle that with Don, Sally, go ahead and put me through." If we put our psychiatrist hat on and analyze this new approach using the transactional analysis model from an earlier chapter we can see that in the former unsuccessful call the child is bleeding through the adult ego state very obviously needy.

It's the difference between being in control or being out of control. In the second example I was choosing to become – tonality wise – parent. Most of the gate keepers will go into adaptive child pretty quick and you will get through. One of the reasons this works is that Sally does not want to make a mistake by keeping someone out that her boss may want to see, like a customer or a vendor or colleague.

A Final Thought on *Being* Versus *Doing*

It is very important to know the difference between who you are and what you do. Shakespeare said that "all the world is a stage and we are merely players". When you are doing your selling job you are in your sales role. Your role as a salesperson is not who you are as a human being it is only one aspect of the many roles you play in life. For example you may be a spouse, child, parent, salesperson, golfer, rotary club member etc. The roles you choose to perform in are infinite and totally up to you. As a human being you are perfect.

Notice that the word *be* is in the word being. We are not called human doings for a reason and the reason is that as a human being you are not defined by the things you do. In sales this concept will make you money and allow you to handle all the rejection that comes your way. If you take rejection personally you are confusing being and doing, who you are with your job role as a salesperson. If you see yourself as less than a ten in your being-ness (and by the way everyone is a ten just because they are alive and human) then you will perform in your selling role as less than ten.

Here is how it works: Joe is an average sales person and he sees himself as a seven on the "Being Scale". Joe's average sale is $1,000, and one day he comes back to the office with a $5,000 sale, or a "ten sale" – a sale five times his average. Joe's manager says "Way to go Joe, fantastic sale!" What do you think Joe says back to the manager? If you said "I got lucky" you would be right.

Let's look at the psychology behind a response like that. Remember Joe sees himself as a seven, but he just made the sale of a ten which is outside his comfort zone of average performance. As a result his internal reasoning goes like this: "I know I'm good, but I am not that good". Assuming Joe believes this, what do you think his future performance will be? Right again, it will go back to the average where Joe's self-image lives and where he is most comfortable. Now let's look at the other side. Joe comes back to the office with a two hundred dollar sale, more the performance of a three. The manager says "Joe your sale is five times below your average, what happened?" Joe says "oh, our price is too high, the economy sucks and I have a bad cold." Looking at the psychology behind this response we find Joe saying internally "I am bad, but I am not that bad" and so he comes up with external reasons for his poor performance, which we also call excuses. If Joe has an external excuse for his performance that is higher than his average and an excuse when his performance is lower than his average you can easily see that Joe fights to stay in his comfort zone at all costs. Keep your psychiatrist hat on for a while longer and think about the following motivational principles:

1. You cannot outperform your self image

2. Your ability usually far exceeds your belief in it

3. Locking yourself into an artificial performance ceiling will cost you lots of money in the long run.

What we have in Joe's case is a self-limiting belief that will cause him to perform at a level far below his capability. I have seen this phenomenon many times with salespeople I have trained.

You have now experienced some powerful sales training assuming you have read the entire book straight through. Open your mind to your unlimited potential. You are a ten and can't get any better as a human being; start to believe this **now**. On the role side you can go as high as you like, it is up to you. When you get into the sales elevator you push the button and go to the floor level that you desire.

If you feel like you're stuck on the fifth floor, all you need to do is get back in the elevator and push ten.

You deserve success and I will see you at the top!

www.ingramcontent.com/pod-product-compliance
Lightning Source LLC
Chambersburg PA
CBHW071618170526
45166CB00003B/1102